THE ROAD.
BURY
BURY
BURY
FIDOS
GRANDMAS
CHOMPERS
DIG DIG DIG
INSERT BONE
GET THE BONE!
PAW-NATURAL
BAKERY
HOWLLL
HOWLIN' FOR HEARTS
PUPTARTS
BONE
BONE
STICK
STONE
ARF ARF
BETTIES PARTY EXPRESS
MUTT MUFFINS
MADE FROM SCRATCH
WHIP ME UP A BATCH OF YER SNICKERPOODLES PLEASE!
BAKIN' DOG
SARAH
DOG
SLIPPER-FULL-O-TRAINING-BITS
BONIFIED 5

Three Dog Bakery™ COOKBOOK

Like everything we do, this effort is
dedicated to all dogs everywhere and to all
the people who love them.

The warmest thanks of all go to all our
wonderful customers, without whom there
would be no Three Dog Bakery.

Three Dog Bakery™

COOKBOOK

Over 50 recipes for all-natural paw-lickin' treats for your dog

Dan Dye & Mark Beckloff

Andrews McMeel Publishing

Kansas City

Final Thoughts

We stand at attention with our ears pulled back in gratitude to Bill Reisler for being the greatest friend our company has ever had. Without this guy, we'd be lost little pups. Thanks, Bill, for everything—the dough, the sound advice and most importantly of all, the great friendship.

Warm pawshakes and wet, slobbery kisses to Ann Willoughby right on her face. Without Ann, God only knows what Three Dog Bakery might look like today. Thanks, Ann, for believing in us right from the start. You're the best.

Thanks to Meg Cundiff, for all the inspired, incredible, wondrous work you do for us. You still the kookiest! Love ya, babe.

Extra treats go to Sue Evins at Quadrillion and Cathryn Wooton for helping to keep this project on schedule. Special thanks to Trish Berlau, our Executive Pastry Chef; Sharon Jordan and Phyllis Dokken, our resident North Dakotans, for all the hard work, testing and double-checking all the recipes. Great job.

Thanks to our entire staff for putting up with us. OUR THREE DOG BAKERY CREW HAS THE HARDEST WORKING BISCUIT BAKERS IN THE KNOWN UNIVERSE! Very hard tail wags to: Our Big Cheese and Head Honcho Top Dog President and CEO:

Ron Butler; V.P. Marketing: Evan Wooton; V.P. Operations: Rocky Valentine; V.P. Finance: Terri Valentine. And the rest of the pack—thanks for everything. All your hard work makes this an extraordinary company! John Escalada, Jeff Schwartz, Diane Fitz, Sandy Brown, Michael Sumstine, Maleah Sumstine, Vivian Perez, William Torres, Federico Arrivillaga, Leonardo Estrada, David Gorrita, Phong Huynh, Thuan Le, Nam Nguyen, Mao Oum, Duy Tran, Thao Nguyen, Nghi Tran, Gisela Estevez, Vidalina Hernandez, Man Ho, Ha Hue La, Anh Le, Bach Le, Huong Nguyen, Lan Tran, Cuong La, Cuong Vo, Chandra Newman, Angela Bell, Jenifer Doleshal, Erin Kelly, Christy Bradburn, Sara Jordan, Bich Nguyen, Nhiem Nguyen.

Thanks to our Board of Directors, and to all of our good friends at PETsMART, Andrews McMeel, Quadrillion Publishing and the fabulous Food Network—especially our executive producer and fellow doglover, Pat O'Gorman.

An extra Sit! Shake! and Rollover! for: LuAnn and Gerald Beckloff, Virgil and Annetta Dye, Richard and Gail Lozoff, Mike Roberts at KCEP, Ann and Jane Rogers in New Orleans, Bonnie Chin and Randy Randolph in Seattle, Bob Bernard and Vince Scannell in Chicago, and The Ewing Kauffman Foundation's Center for Entrepreneurial Leadership.

PROJECT EDITOR—SUZANNE EVINS
DESIGN MANAGER—JUSTINA LEITÃO
DESIGN—MARK BUCKINGHAM
ILLUSTRATOR—MEG CUNDIFF
FOOD PHOTOGRAPHY—NEIL SUTHERLAND
DOG PHOTOGRAPHY—TIM POTT & TATJANA ALVEGAARD
HOME ECONOMIST—KATHRYN HAWKINS
COMMISSIONING EDITOR—WILL STEEDS
PRODUCTION—NEIL RANDLES, KAREN STAFF & RUTH ARTHUR

WWW.ANDREWSMCMEEL.COM

LIBRARY OF CONGRESS CATALOGING-IN-PUBLICATION NUMBER: 98-7836

ISBN 0-8362-6919-5

ATTENTION: SCHOOLS AND BUSINESSES

ANDREWS MCMEEL BOOKS ARE AVAILABLE AT QUANTITY DISCOUNTS WITH BULK PURCHASE FOR EDUCATIONAL, BUSINESS, OR SALES PROMOTIONAL USE. FOR INFORMATION, PLEASE WRITE TO: SPECIAL SALES DEPARTMENT, ANDREWS MCMEEL PUBLISHING, 4520 MAIN STREET, KANSAS CITY, MISSOURI 64111.

Contents

Remember, although a dog's idea of nirvana is to eat like this every day, the recipes in
this cookbook should be considered supplements to your dog's regular diet, not replacements.
Consult your vet if you have any questions regarding a particular recipe for your dog.

Welcome to Three Dog Bakery ...

the world's original bakery for dogs!

THE BAKERY IS NOW OPEN!

Attention! Calling all dogs! Calling all dog lovers!
Welcome to Three Dog Bakery, the world's first bone-i-fied, five-paw bakery ... for dogs! First off, let us woof from the roof, that anyone buying this book is entitled to many warm pawshakes, cold noses and vigorous tail wags from all of us here at Three Dog Bakery. Chances are, if you are holding this book in your paws, you probably love dogs as much as we do. Dogs are truly what it's all about for us. We love dogs! And dogs love us!

The recipes that we have compiled here represent a grand Four-Paws-Up assortment of great tasting, easy-to-make treats that you can bake at home for your dog. We've tried to keep the techniques very simple so that everyone can feel comfortable, regardless of your culinary abilities. We also spent extra time selecting easy-to-find ingredients for the recipes ... you'll be able to find most, if not all, of them right in your own kitchen. We want your baking-for-dogs experience to be a fun, fur-filled fiesta.

Cooking for your dog strengthens the bonds of commitment and devotion that you already share with your pup—especially as we all know the quickest way to a dog's heart is through his stomach! In the following pages, you'll discover an incredible selection of appetizers, sweet treats, savory snacks, celebration goodies, treats for the holidays, even some dinner recipes—all guaranteed to send your dog's tail into a happy, hungry, full throttle. Bone appetit—from the Three Dog Bakery kitchens to yours!

We'd like to shake your paw

There are lots of ways in which you may already be familiar with us. Perhaps you've already visited one of our bakeries; or you've enjoyed our first book, *Short Tails and Treats from Three Dog Bakery*, which chronicled the "tail" of how we started and grew our business; or maybe you've caught our weekly cooking show on the Food Network. In case this is your first encounter with our company, we are the founders of Three Dog Bakery, quite pawsibly the world's most unique bakery. We're the bakery that is soon to be famous the world rover. Behind the Three Dog Bakery name, baking and barking at our sides every step of the way, have been the

three very cute and very hungry founding sisters of the bakery, who are fast becoming celebri-dogs in their own right. No matter where we travel to in this great country of ours, from NYC to Seattle, the girls are always recognized … usually way before we are. Come here, girls! Let everyone meet you.

First we have **Sarah Jean, the Biscuit Queen,** who is a very sweet, very smart, very nosey, 10½-year-old black Lab mix. Next, we have her little sister, a 10-year-old Dalmatian, **Dottie** (aka Spots Galore) who is very lovable, very cuddly and very sleepy (not necessarily in that order). Finally, there is the precious baby, **Gracie,** a magnificent, noble, clumsy, kooky 9-year-old albino Great Dane who was born deaf and who casts her enchanting spell over everyone she meets.

Our customers are amazed and delighted that our company was actually named after honest-to-goodness, real, live, great dogs and not as a result of a marketing gimmick dreamed up at some ad agency. Obviously, nobody's happier about our name than Sarah, Dottie and Gracie themselves … big hams.

The girls have been instrumental in shaping our company into what it is today. They have selflessly served the company in many capacities over the past eight years. We could not have survived without their long years of bone-weary duty as Official Taste Testers, Customer Greeters, Delivery Driver Sniffers, Trash Diggers, Floor Cleaners, Product Demonstrators and Exit Blockers (believe us, it can really help sales to have a 150 pound Great Dane block the exit). Sarah, Dottie

and Gracie's collective years (and we're talking dog years here) of working like dogs, their dogged determination, their endless tail-wagging and even their occasional growling at bill collectors, have served as motivation and inspiration for us all. Thanks, girls.

A fun-lovin', dog-lovin' company

One of the things we love most of all is meeting our customers and listening to their comments and stories. Some questions seem to crop up over and over again, like, "Why on earth did you start a bakery for dogs?" The answer is as pure and simple today as it was when we started out back in 1989. We pawsitively, absolutely, truly, totally, completely love dogs. We've both shared a deep love for dogs our entire lives. We also desperately wanted to liberate ourselves from the cold, uncaring, dog-eat-dog corporate world. We knew that if we were to start a business and if it was to be successful, it had to be centered around something we both truly loved. For that reason, we knew it had to involve dogs.

By happy coincidence, Mark's mom, LuAnn, had given him a bone-shaped biscuit cutter in his Christmas stocking that year as a gag gift, knowing how much he loved dogs. Little could she have known what she had unleashed! The proverbial light bulb lit up over both our heads as the idea washed over us: we could start baking dog biscuits. We would make the best dog biscuits on the planet! The more we thought about our idea the more excited we became. We would use only delicious, all-natural ingredients—stuff we'd feel great about eating ourselves. We began to research and find out what kinds of ingredients to put in the World's Best Dog Biscuit and what things to stay away from. We got advice from vets, breeders, dog lovers, pet shop owners and, of course, lots and lots of dogs.

As we began our research, we thought it was creepy to read ingredient labels on store-bought dog biscuits and sometimes find 50 different ingredients listed—for a simple dog bone! It seemed 40 of those ingredients we couldn't even pronounce, let alone know why they were there in the first place. How could we look Sarah, Dottie and Gracie in the eye and explain to them that the biscuits they were eating had a longer shelf-life than they did? Everything was full of chemicals, preservatives and God only knows what else. Saddest of all, these so-called "treats" were guilty of the ultimate, most heinous crime in our eyes: they were boring … we mean boring! The same old beef, chicken, liver blah blah blah. It was just arf-ul. It seemed to us that dogs were fun! Dogs wanted to have fun! And that meant that dogs needed fun treats immediately! It became our mission, our personal crusade, to see that they got them.

For months we experimented out of our kitchen at home. We burnt ourselves. We burnt our biscuits. We had cookies that curled, bubbled, cracked, molded, crumbled, split and everything in between. Finally, we arrived at the perfect cookie: golden, flavorful, crunchy. It was perfect. The girls couldn't get enough of them. Neither could our neighbor's dogs or our co-worker's dogs. Everyone began urging us to sell them. We began to go out on our lunch breaks from our "real" jobs (I was a copywriter and Mark was in accounting) to find accounts that might carry our treats. We began selling our unique fresh-baked treats to pet stores, health food stores and to veterinarians who loved the fact that they could eat them themselves! We tried to find as many accounts as we could. Soon we were quite out of control, constantly expanding our baking re"pet"oire with fun, original flavors, developing great-tasting additional treats, finding new accounts and creating exciting ways for folks to celebrate their dogs.

Giving the term "baked from scratch" a whole new meaning

Soon we decided that in addition to wholesaling, it would be fun to provide a way for our customers to come in and buy our biscuits hot and fresh—straight out of the oven—in a dog-friendly bakery setting. We were already developing a very loyal customer base. So we moved our baking operation out of the house and opened our first retail bakery location in Kansas City, Missouri. After a year we outgrew it and moved up to a

bigger space in a higher rent district. Soon we outgrew that as well. We moved up again. Dogs were barking the news to other dogs. The word was out on the streets … and dogs were howling for more!

As our business continued to expand, we scratched out new accounts. We were growing in our ability to sell to big national accounts. Our yummy Three Dog Bakery brand began showing up in the upscale Neiman Marcus stores, Hallmark and PETsMART stores worldwide, along with other quality-conscious national chains. We also began offering and shipping our treats nationwide through the mail with our own shop-at-home DOGalog®—sorry to all the kitties out there … no cat-alogs for us! (And what an ultimate irony … the mailman delivering dog treats! It must be some sort of poetic justice.)

We know it's hard sometimes for people to understand what a bakery for dogs is all about. Just for the record, our stores are full-service, full-line, fully-working bakeries. The only difference is most of our

customers have four legs instead of two, drool alot and show a marked propensity for eating off the floor … and sometimes peeing there, too. (Not that those kinds of activities don't occur from time to time in "human" bakeries!) Our chain of dog-lovin' bakeries are true meccas for munching mongrels. Think of them as Pooch Patisseries, Canine Confectioneries—hot spots where dogs go to see and be seen, sniff and be sniffed, nibble and be nibbled. It's great fun to watch dogs come in, straining at the leash, dragging in their humans. What a delight to watch dogs eagerly begin sniffing around for their own treats—everything from our luscious fresh-baked PupCakes® and Rollovers® to Great Danish® and tasty Bark 'n Fetch™ Biscuits. Imagine the fun of snooping out over 100 wholesome treats you'll find only inside a Three Dog Bakery.

Happy tails to you

Even after all these years, there's still nothing that we love more than cooking up fresh, wholesome, healthy treats for dogs. Everything we create at Three Dog is made without adding salt, sugar, artificial ingredients, chemicals or unnecessary fats and oils. We use only simple ingredients … close-to-the-earth grains, herbs, fruits and vegetables—

flavors that dogs love and that you as a pet owner can understand. That's important to us. Over the years we have continued to refine and define our concept, listening carefully to our customers.

Mark → Dan

Gracie Sarah Dottie

Today, as we are opening bakeries all across America, our mission still remains the same—to bake the best dog treats on the planet and get them to as many dogs as possible!

Happy baking! And barking!

If your dogs are like Sarah, Dottie and Gracie, they need an appetizer to awaken their palette about as much as Barbra Streisand needs a singing lesson! But if you're having a party, remember that success is in the de"tails", and don't forget to include the four-legged party animals, too. It's fun to serve your dogs a treat made especially for them. Any of these tail-wagging recipes can be made ahead and served with much gusto at your next pawty.

Get down! Off that couch!

GRRRRRRRANOLA

Makes a grrrrrrreat big Grrrrrrreat Dane-sized portion

ISN'T IT FUNNY HOW A DOG LOVES HONEY? NUTTY, ALL NATURAL, MIXED FLAVORS FOR
YOUR NUTTY, ALL-NATURAL, MIXED BREED (OR PEDIGREE!)

¾ cup honey

½ cup vegetable oil

1 teaspoon vanilla

2 cups cracked wheat

2½ cups rolled oats

2 cups bran flakes

1 cup wheat germ

1 cup sunflower seeds

1 cup chopped roasted soybeans

- Preheat oven to 325 degrees.

- Heat honey, oil and vanilla in a saucepan.

- Pour over all the dry ingredients in a bowl. Mix thoroughly and spread on two greased baking sheets.

- Bake for 15 minutes or until nicely golden brown. Stir occasionally during baking to prevent overbrowning.

- Cool and store in a sealed container.

BISCUIT BITES

Makes 20 vampishly vonderful biscuits

JUST A LITTLE MOUTHWATERING GARLIC KEEPS THE VAMPIRES AWAY. WHAT DOG WOULDN'T GO BATTY FOR THESE TEMPTING LITTLE SNACKS?

BISCUITS:

2 cups white flour

3 teaspoons baking powder

¼ cup vegetable shortening

⅔ cup skim milk

TOPPING:

8 ounces low-fat cream cheese

4 ounces mushrooms, finely chopped

½ teaspoon minced garlic

2 teaspoons parsley

- Preheat oven to 450 degrees. Sift flour and baking powder into a bowl. Cut shortening into flour until the mixture looks like coarse crumbs.

- Add milk and stir with a fork until a dough forms. Turn onto a floured surface and knead 10 to 20 strokes.

- Roll out dough ½-inch thick, cut out circles with a biscuit cutter and place biscuits on an ungreased cookie sheet.

- To make the topping, mix all ingredients together in a bowl and put about a teaspoon of topping mixture on each biscuit.

- Bake for 12 to 15 minutes. Cool on a rack and serve. Store leftovers in a sealed container in the refrigerator.

Watch Your Step

DoTTie

The world's smallest dog was a Yorkshire terrier who stood 2¹/₂ inches and measured 3³/₄ inches from nose to tail. He weighed 4 ounces, which would have made him a crouton-sized companion for the world's heaviest dog, a 343 pound Old English Mastiff.

SALIVATIN' SALMON ROLL

Slices up into 8 fantastically fishy, catch-of-the-day snacks

YOUR DOG'S GONNA BE HOOKED! WHAT A CATCH THIS
SIMPLE RECIPE IS—IN FACT, IT'S REEL TASTY!

2 cups canned salmon

8 ounces low-fat cream cheese

2 teaspoons minced garlic

$\frac{1}{4}$ teaspoon beef broth

$\frac{1}{2}$ cup chopped pecans

1 tablespoon chopped fresh parsley

- Drain and flake salmon, removing any skin and bones.

- Combine salmon, cream cheese, garlic and beef broth. Chill this mixture at least 1 hour.

- Shape salmon mixture into a 2 x 8-inch log and roll in pecans and parsley.

- Slice into 8 pieces and serve. Store in a sealed container in the refrigerator.

CHEESY APPLE NIPS

Makes 16 wonderful, wagging wedges

A HANDPICKED FAVORITE! THESE CHEESY-TO-THE-CORE TREATS ARE
CRUNCHILY PERFECT FOR THE APPLE OF YOUR EYE

3 ounces low-fat cream cheese

2 ounces blue cheese

4 medium apples

- Beat cream cheese and blue cheese together until smooth.

- Core apples and fill with cheese mixture.

- Chill for 2 to 3 hours.

- Cut into wedges to serve. Store in a sealed container in the refrigerator.

SCRUMPTIOUS SCOTTIE SCONES

Makes approximately 25 sweet and savory scones

AFTER A MORNING OF SNOOZING IN THE SUN, THIS IS WHAT THE
WELL TURNED-OUT DOG TRULY ADORES FOR AFTERNOON TEA

2 cups white flour

2 teaspoons baking powder

1 tablespoon honey

¼ cup vegetable oil

1 egg

½ cup skim milk

1 clove garlic, minced

- Preheat oven to 350 degrees.

- Combine flour, baking powder and honey in a bowl. Add oil, egg, milk and garlic, then stir until mixed thoroughly.

- Turn out dough onto a lightly floured surface and knead.

- Roll out to ½-inch thick, cut into 2-inch squares and place on a greased baking sheet.

- Bake for 15 minutes, allow to cool on a rack then serve. Store in an airtight container.

CHEESE PLEASE HOUND ROUNDS

Bakes up approximately 24 chewy, cheesy chompers

YOUR HOUND WILL DEFINITELY HANG AROUND
WHEN HE SMELLS THESE ROUNDS!

2 cups white flour
½ cup shredded low-fat Cheddar cheese
½ cup low-fat cottage cheese
1 teaspoon chopped cilantro leaves
1 teaspoon parsley flakes
2 tablespoons vegetable oil
¾ cup chopped peanuts
⅔ cup water

- Preheat oven to 375 degrees.
- Mix together flour, Cheddar and cottage cheese, cilantro leaves and parsley.
- Add oil, peanuts and water and mix thoroughly.
- Break off golf ball-size pieces and shape into balls.
- Place on a greased baking sheet and bake for 30 minutes. Cool on a rack and serve. Store in a sealed container in the refrigerator.

Pup-ular Herbs

Alfalfa: aids in healing allergies, stomach ailments and treats bad breath.

Garlic: a natural flea repellent.

Oregano: helps digestion.

Parsley: helps sweeten breath.

POOCHIE PLEASIN' PRETZELS

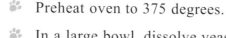

Makes 10 to 12 paw-licking pretzels

WHEN YOUR POOCH NEEDS TREATS IN A HURRY, DON'T GET TWISTED ... TWIST UP SOME OF THESE INSTEAD!

1 package active dry yeast

1½ cups warm water (110–115 degrees)

1 tablespoon honey

4 cups white flour

1 egg, beaten

- Preheat oven to 375 degrees.

- In a large bowl, dissolve yeast in warm water. Add honey and enough flour to make a soft dough and knead for 6 to 8 minutes until smooth.

- Pinch off about 2 tablespoons of dough for each pretzel. Roll out dough using the palm of your hand into long, pencil-like shapes, about 12 inches long and ½-inch thick.

- Shape into pretzel twists and place on a greased baking sheet. Brush with beaten egg. Bake for 20 minutes, then cool on a rack. Store leftovers in a sealed container.

CORGI CRUMPETS

Makes approximately 24 mouthwatering jewels

TREAT LOYALTY WITH A GRAND BIT OF ROYALTY. THIS IS THE PERFECT SNACK FOR THOSE TIMES WHEN YOUR LITTLE PRINCESS DEMANDS THE VERY BEST!

2½ cups cornmeal

1½ cups white flour

2 tablespoons vegetable oil

1 egg

¾ cup honey

½ teaspoon baking powder

1⅓ cups water

- Preheat oven to 350 degrees.

- Mix all ingredients together thoroughly.

- Spoon into muffin pans three-quarters full.

- Bake for 35 minutes then cool on a rack and serve. Store in an airtight container.

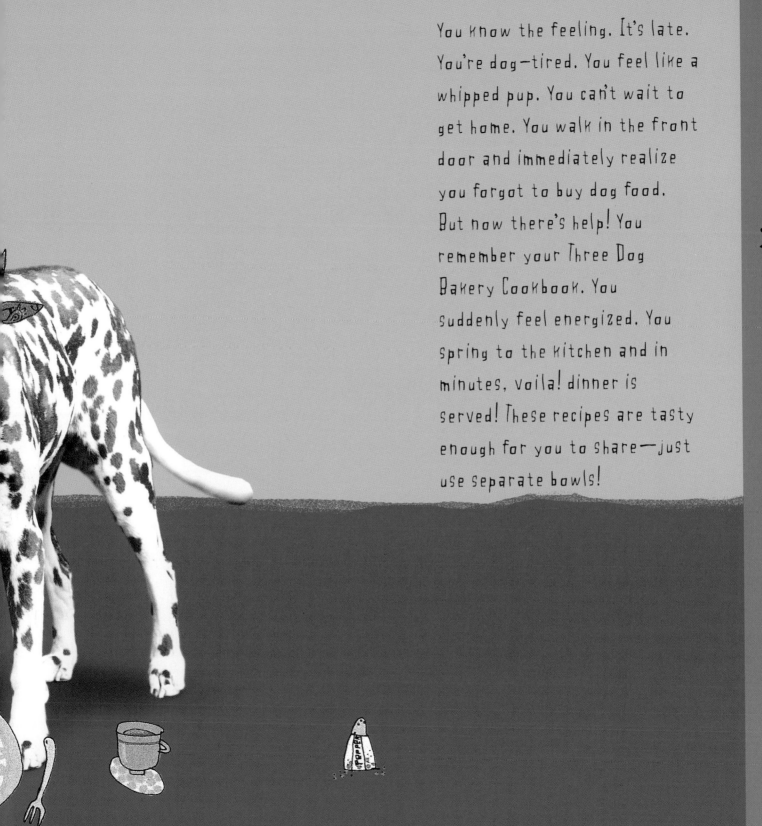

You know the feeling. It's late. You're dog-tired. You feel like a whipped pup. You can't wait to get home. You walk in the front door and immediately realize you forgot to buy dog food. But now there's help! You remember your Three Dog Bakery Cookbook. You suddenly feel energized. You spring to the kitchen and in minutes, voila! dinner is served! These recipes are tasty enough for you to share—just use separate bowls!

Woof-it-Down Vittles

GERMAN SHEPHERD'S PIE

Bakes up into an incredibly tasty 10-inch pie

WE HAVEN'T FOUND A DOG YET WHO DOESN'T LOVE TO
GOBBLE, GOBBLE, GOBBLE THIS TANTALIZING TURKEY PIE

1 cup cooked ground turkey

1 cup shredded low-fat
Cheddar cheese

1 clove garlic, minced

3 tablespoons chopped
green bell pepper

3 tablespoons chopped
red bell pepper

1 cup skim milk

¼ cup white flour

2 eggs

Preheat oven to 375 degrees.

In a 10-inch pie pan, layer the ground turkey, cheese, garlic and peppers.

In a separate bowl, stir together milk, flour and eggs.

Pour over meat and cheese layers, but do not stir.

Bake for 30 minutes. When pie is cooled, cut into wedges and serve. Store in the refrigerator.

CHICKEN CAT-CHIATORE

Makes 8 purr-fectly sized servings

HARD TO BELIEVE, BUT DOGS PREFER CHICKEN OVER KITTENS! YOUR HUNGRY PUP WILL THINK THIS IS THE CAT'S MEOW

2 pounds chicken, cooked and chopped, bones removed

2 cloves garlic, minced

8 ounces tomato sauce

3 tomatoes, chopped

1 teaspoon oregano

2 bay leaves

½ teaspoon basil

🐾 Combine all ingredients except chicken in a covered skillet. Stir and simmer gently for 1 hour.

🐾 Add chicken after the hour and simmer for an additional 20 minutes.

🐾 Cool slightly, then serve over a bed of vermicelli, egg noodles or white rice. Store leftovers in a doggie bag in the refrigerator.

Man's Oldest Friend?

Dogs, or their wolf ancestors, could have been domesticated as long ago as 135,000 years— not the mere 14,000 years as long believed. The oldest existing breeds are the dingo, the African basenji, the greyhound and the New Guinea singing dog.

LAZY DAY LOAF

Makes 8 servings, depending on the size of your little lazy bones

A PERFECTLY EASY-TO-MAKE (EASIER TO EAT!) DINNER WHEN YOU DON'T FEEL LIKE LIFTING A PAW

1 pound ground turkey

2 eggs

⅛ cup skim milk

1½ cups bread crumbs

10 ounces frozen chopped spinach, thawed and drained

4 ounces low-fat Cheddar cheese, cubed

- Preheat oven to 350 degrees.

- Mix together meat, eggs, milk and bread crumbs.

- Put half the mixture in a greased loaf pan.

- Layer spinach and cheese in the middle, and top with the other half of the meat mixture.

- Bake for 1½ hours or until done. Store in the refrigerator.

LABRADOR LASAGNA

Makes 10 tasty rollovers

OODLES AND OODLES OF NOODLES FOR LABRADORS TO POODLES

10 lasagna noodles, cooked

1 cup low-fat cottage cheese

1 cup frozen chopped spinach, thawed and drained

1½ cups skim milk

2 tablespoons white flour

¼ cup chopped tomato

½ teaspoon minced garlic

½ teaspoon oregano

- Preheat oven to 350 degrees.

- In a bowl, combine cottage cheese and spinach.

- Take each lasagna noodle and spread 2 tablespoons of cottage cheese mixture along the inside of the noodle, then roll up each one. Place in a 9 x 13-inch greased baking pan and set aside.

- Mix flour and milk in a covered container and shake until blended. Place in a small saucepan over medium heat and stir constantly until slightly thickened. Add tomato and garlic.

- Pour the sauce over rolled up noodles and garnish with oregano. Bake for 20 minutes, then cool before serving. Store any leftovers in the refrigerator.

JEWELS OF THE SEA JUBILEE

Yields 9 squares of deep sea treasure

YOU DON'T HAVE TO BE A SALTY SEA DOG TO
APPRECIATE THESE SEA-SONED SNACKS

1 clove garlic, minced

1 cup shrimp, cooked and chopped

1 cup crab, cookcd and chopped

½ cup chopped celery

8 ounces low-fat cream cheese

1 cup dry bread crumbs

½ cup chopped green bell pepper

1 egg, beaten

- Preheat oven to 350 degrees.

- Mix all ingredients together thoroughly.

- Spread mixture in an 8 x 8-inch square pan.

- Bake for 1 hour, then cool and cut into 9 squares. Store any leftovers in the refrigerator.

HEARTY HOUND LOAF

Makes 8 portions, depending on the size of your dog's tank

ONE, TWO, CHEW A SHOE. THREE, FOUR, SCRATCH THE DOOR. FIVE, SIX, LEARNING TRICKS. WHEW—IT'S HARD, HUNGRY WORK BEING A DOG!

1½ pounds ground turkey

1 egg

1 cup cornmeal

½ teaspoon sage

1 tablespoon minced garlic

¼ cup finely chopped green bell pepper

½ cup corn

1 medium tomato, chopped

6 ounces tomato paste

- Preheat oven to 350 degrees.
- Combine all ingredients in a large bowl and mix well.
- Pack into a greased loaf pan and bake for 1½ hours.
- Cool, slice and serve. Store any unused portions in the refrigerator.

No Gracias, We'll Pass

The chihuahua is named after the state of Chihuahua in Mexico. These little critters were considered sacred by the Aztec Indians and were sometimes eaten during their religious ceremonies.

Seconds, anyone?

HUNGRY MONGREL TURKEY BURGERS

Makes 8 to 10 juicy burgers—grilled or fried, you decide

WATCH WITH EAGLE-EYED PRECISION WHILE COOKING.
YOUR DOG WON'T WAIT TO GET HIS PAWS ON THESE!

1½ pounds ground turkey
2 egg yolks
2 tablespoons parsley flakes
1 tablespoon minced garlic
¼ teaspoon thyme
½ cup dry bread crumbs
½ cup cooked rice

- Combine all ingredients in a bowl and mix thoroughly.
- Leave to chill in the refrigerator for at least 1 hour.
- Shape into patties and broil in the oven for about 15 to 20 minutes until burger is no longer pink in the middle. Turn after one side is well browned.
- Cool and serve. Store in a sealed container in the refrigerator.

CHOW ITALIANO

Makes 12 servings—enough for guests Paw-varotti and Maria Collies

MAMA MIA! WITH THESE ON THE MENU YOUR
PUP WON'T WANT TO ROME

8 ounces thin spaghetti or similar pasta
2 eggs, beaten
½ cup skim milk
8 ounces tomato sauce
½ cup water
4 ounces low-fat mozzarella cheese, shredded

- Preheat oven to 350 degrees.
- Cook spaghetti, drain and rinse in hot water.
- Toss with beaten egg and milk then stir in tomato sauce and water.
- Pour into a 9 x 13-inch greased pan and sprinkle cheese on top. Bake for 45 minutes.
- Cool, cut into squares and serve. Store leftovers in a sealed container and refrigerate.

CHOWDOWN CHEESY CASSEROLE

Makes 4 gooey, cheesy, noodley servings

TURKEY! CHEESE! PASTA! THINK YOUR DOG'S GONNA SHARE WITH YOU?
NO NEED TO WASH THE PLATE ... IT'LL BE LICKED CLEAN!

1½ pounds ground turkey, cooked

3 8-ounce cans tomato sauce

2 cups water

½ teaspoon minced garlic

½ teaspoon oregano

1 cup shredded low-fat Cheddar cheese

8 ounces egg noodles

8 ounces low-fat mozzarella cheese, shredded

- Preheat oven to 350 degrees.

- Place all ingredients, except mozzarella cheese, in a large bowl and stir, mixing thoroughly.

- Pour into an 8-inch greased baking pan and bake for 50 minutes.

- Top with mozzarella cheese and bake an additional 10 minutes. Cool slightly before serving. Refrigerate any unused portion promptly in a covered container.

GRACIE'S SLOBBER GOBBLER LOAF

Makes 6 Great Dane-sized slices

WHEN IT COMES TO FOOD, MORE IS ALWAYS, ALWAYS BETTER. JUST ASK GRACIE!

2 pounds ground turkey

2 tablespoons minced garlic

1 egg

½ cup quick-cook barley

1 cup quick-cook oats

6 ounces tomato paste

½ tablespoon parsley flakes

- Preheat oven to 350 degrees.

- In a mixing bowl, combine turkey, garlic, egg, barley and oats. Mix thoroughly.

- Spoon into a greased loaf pan and pat down meat mixture until level.

- Spread tomato paste on top of the loaf and sprinkle with parsley.

- Bake for 1 to 1¼ hours. Cool and cut into 6 even slices. Store unused portion wrapped in the refrigerator.

And the Title Goes to . . .

The top six most pup-ular breeds in America are:

Labrador Retriever
Rottweiler
German Shepherd
Golden Retriever
Beagle
Poodle

It's not exactly a newsflash to report that dogs love sweets! Who hasn't come home to find the candy bowl empty, scraps of foil lying on the floor and two very guilty eyes staring at you? Be very careful—the wrong treats can be extremely dangerous to your pups. At Three Dog Bakery, we lightly sweeten some of our treats with fruits, vegetables or maybe a touch of honey or carob. This way we can satisfy your hound's sweet tooth— the natural way.

Sweets for the Sweet

OATMEAL PUREBRED BREAD

Bakes up 12 slices of haute oat heaven

PURE, SIMPLE AND WHOLESOME. WITH INGREDIENTS THIS GREAT,
IT "OAT" TO BE DELICIOUS!

2 packages active dry yeast
½ cup warm water
1½ cups boiling water
1 cup quick-cook oats
½ cup molasses
⅓ cup vegetable shortening
6 cups white flour
2 eggs, beaten

- Dissolve yeast in ½ cup warm water.

- Combine 1½ cups boiling water, oats, molasses, and shortening in a large bowl. Cool to lukewarm and stir in half the flour (3 cups).

- Add eggs and stir the mixture thoroughly. Stir in yeast and add the remaining 3 cups flour. Mix well, cover tightly, and place in the refrigerator overnight.

- Turn onto a well-floured surface and shape into two loaves. Place in greased loaf pans and cover with a clean towel. Leave to rise in a warm place for about 2 hours until double in size.

- Preheat oven to 375 degrees.

- Bake for 45 minutes, then allow to cool and slice. Store in a sealed container.

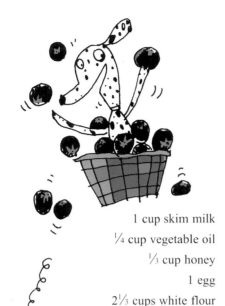

BLUE BLUE BERRY BERRY BUN BUNS

Makes a dozen berry, berry delicious muffins

THROW IN SOME EXTRA BLUEBERRIES TO MAKE THEM
EXTRA SPOTTED … JUST LIKE DOTTIE!

1 cup skim milk

¼ cup vegetable oil

⅓ cup honey

1 egg

2⅓ cups white flour

4 teaspoons baking powder

1 teaspoon vanilla

1½ cups fresh blueberries

- Preheat oven to 375 degrees.

- In mixing bowl, combine milk, oil and honey. Add egg and blend well.

- Combine flour and baking powder in a separate bowl and add to wet ingredients. Stir together thoroughly.

- Add vanilla and fold in blueberries.

- Grease a muffin tin and fill two-thirds full.

- Bake for 20 to 25 minutes, or until a toothpick inserted in the center of a muffin comes out clean. Cool before serving and store in a sealed container.

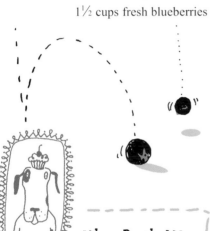

It's a Dog's Life

The US has the largest
pup-ulation with about
58 million dogs.
There are 700 breeds worldwide, with a total dog
pup-ulation of over 100 million.
France has the second largest
population of dogs, and Japan
has the fastest growing.

GRANDPAW'S SPICE COOKIES

Makes approximately 25 golden-baked, paw-natural cookies

YUM ... REMEMBER THE TRIPS TO GRANDMA AND
GRANDPAW'S WHEN YOU WERE A PUP?

½ cup honey
¾ cup unsweetened applesauce
¼ cup molasses
1 egg
2¼ cups white flour
2 teaspoons baking soda
1 teaspoon ginger
1 teaspoon cinnamon
½ teaspoon ground cloves
½ cup chopped peanuts

- Preheat oven to 350 degrees.

- Mix together honey, applesauce, molasses and egg in a bowl.

- In a separate bowl, combine flour, baking soda and spices, then stir into the molasses mixture.

- Drop teaspoonfuls of the mixture onto a greased baking sheet. Sprinkle a few peanuts on top and pat down gently with your hand.

- Bake for 8 to 10 minutes then cool on a rack before serving. Store in an airtight container.

BARKIN' BREAD

Makes up to 16 pieces ... more than enough to fill a doggie bag

FRESH-BAKED BREAD THIS GOOD IS DEFINITELY
WORTH BARKING ABOUT

¾ cup vegetable oil
½ cup honey
1 egg
2 cups grated squash
2½ cups white flour
1 teaspoon baking soda
½ teaspoon baking powder
3 teaspoons cinnamon
½ cup chopped walnuts

- Preheat oven to 350 degrees.

- In a large bowl, mix oil, honey and egg, then add grated squash.

- Sift flour, baking soda, baking powder and cinnamon into the other ingredients. Add nuts and stir thoroughly until well mixed.

- Pour into a greased loaf pan and bake for 45 minutes, then cool and serve in slices. Store in an airtight container.

COLD NOSE COCO LOCO BARK BARS

Makes 12 dreamy, drooly, delicious bars

TALK ABOUT BARKING UP THE RIGHT TREE ... THE FRUIT TREE! WHAT A FRUITY WAY TO START YOUR DOG'S DAY—HE'S GONNA GO LOCO FOR THESE FRUITY TREATS

7 ounces canned unsweetened fruit cocktail

⅜ cup honey

1 egg

½ teaspoon vanilla

1⅛ cups white flour

¾ teaspoon baking soda

½ cup unsweetened shredded coconut

¼ cup chopped walnuts

- Preheat oven to 350 degrees.

- Drain fruit cocktail and set aside.

- In a large bowl, combine honey and eggs. Add fruit cocktail and vanilla and mix thoroughly.

- Combine the flour and baking soda in a separate bowl, then add this to the wet mixture and stir well.

- Pour into a 8 x 8-inch greased baking pan and sprinkle the top with coconut and walnuts.

- Bake for 20 to 25 minutes, then cool and cut into bars. Store in a sealed container.

HOWLIN' HULA COOKIES

Makes 20 tropical treats—more than enough for a Labrador luau

HU-LA-LA! WITH A BELLY FULL OF THESE TASTE-OF-PARADISE TREATS, YOUR DOG WILL WANT TO LEI DOWN AND DREAM OF A THATCHED DOG HUT IN THE ISLANDS

8 ounces canned unsweetened
crushed pineapple
¼ cup vegetable oil
¼ cup honey
1 egg
1 teaspoon vanilla
2 cups white flour
1½ teaspoons baking powder
¼ teaspoon baking soda

- Preheat oven to 350 degrees.

- Drain pineapple and set aside.

- In a mixing bowl, combine oil and honey. Add egg, pineapple and vanilla and mix thoroughly.

- Combine flour, baking powder and baking soda in a separate bowl. After blending, add this into the wet mixture and stir well.

- Drop tablespoonfuls of the mixture onto a greased baking sheet and bake for 20 minutes. Cool on a rack, then serve. Store in an airtight container.

The Breed, the Greed, the Deed

The richest dog in America was Toby, a poodle who was left $15 million by his owner in 1931. Sadly, the executors couldn't wait to get their paws on the dough, so Toby was hastened to the Great Kennel in the Sky.

39

BARKERY-FRESH CAROB CAKES

Bakes a dozen decadently delicious cakes

WATCH YOUR FINGERS WHILE SERVING!

½ cup honey

2 cups white flour

½ cup low-fat mayonnaise

3 tablespoons carob powder

2 teaspoons baking soda

1 cup warm water

1 teaspoon vanilla

- Preheat oven to 350 degrees.
- Blend together all ingredients very thoroughly.
- Grease a muffin tin and fill each tin half full with the mixture.
- Bake for 25 minutes or until a toothpick comes out clean when inserted in the middle of a muffin.
- Cool and store in a sealed container.

SHAR-PIE

Makes 4 individual pies—one for each paw!

WE'VE IRONED THE WRINKLES OUT OF THIS RECIPE FOR YOUR LITTLE SWEETIE PIE!

FILLING:

1 large sweet potato

⅛ cup honey

1 egg

pinch of nutmeg

pinch of cinnamon

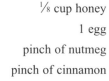

CRUST:

1½ cups white flour

¼ cup honey

¼ cup vegetable shortening

3–4 tablespoons iced water

- Preheat oven to 350 degrees.
- Cook sweet potato by baking for approximately 60 minutes. When potato has cooled, peel off skin.
- Mix sweet potato with honey, egg, nutmeg and cinnamon, and set aside.
- To make the crust, cut shortening into white flour and honey until crumbly.
- Add iced water 1 tablespoon at a time until mixture binds together. Knead until smooth. Roll out dough and cut four 5-inch circles to form crusts in 4-inch foil pie pans.
- Pour sweet potato mixture into crusts and bake for 25 minutes. Cool before serving. Store well wrapped in the refrigerator.

LAZY BONES CAROB BALLS

Makes 20 balls ... so easy, they almost make themselves

THE EASY AND DELICIOUS CHOICE FOR THOSE NON-WORKING BREEDS

1 cup carob powder

1 cup skim milk

2 tablespoons honey

1 teaspoon vanilla

3 cups bran flake cereal

- In a large bowl, combine carob, milk, honey and vanilla.

- Add bran flakes and mix thoroughly.

- Break off golf ball-size pieces and form into balls.

- Place balls in a sealed container and refrigerate for at least 1 hour before serving.

- Store remaining balls in an airtight container in the refrigerator.

BANANA MUTT COOKIES

Makes about 20 mutt pleasers

WHEW! CAT CHASING CAN BE EXHAUSTING WORK—THIS IS TRULY THE PAWS THAT REFRESHES. USE FRESH BANANAS AND YOUR DOGS WILL LOVE YOU A BUNCH!

1½ cups ripe mashed bananas
½ teaspoon vanilla
3 cups oats
½ cup chopped peanuts
¼ cup applesauce

- Preheat oven to 350 degrees.

- Mix all ingredients together thoroughly.

- Drop spoonfuls of the mixture onto an ungreased baking sheet, and press flat with a fork.

- Bake for approximately 15 minutes, then cool on a rack before serving. Store in an airtight container.

Let Sleeping Dogs Lie

Ever wondered why a dog circles before lying down? In the wild, circling was a way of preparing a sleeping area, flattening down tall grasses. It would also serve as a scent barrier, to ensure others knew that an area was taken.

Dogs live through their senses—especially their sense of smell. Some researchers think a dog's sense of smell may be a million times keener than our own. So be prepared to witness your pooch enter a zombie-like, tail-wagging delirium when the aroma of these savory snacks starts wafting out of the kitchen. If you live near other dogs, you may want to double the recipe—or face the consequences. It could be mutiny on the bone-ty!

WOOF WOOF WAFFLES

Makes 12 tail-waggin' waffles

NO NEED TO WAFFLE ON THIS ONE—WOOF THESE DOWN HOWL!

4 cups whole-wheat flour
½ cup cornmeal
1 egg
2 tablespoons vegetable oil
1¾ cups water

- Preheat oven to 325 degrees.

- Mix all ingredients together then turn out onto a lightly floured surface and knead well.

- Roll out dough to ½-inch thick and cut out 8-inch squares.

- Place each square on a waffle iron (unplugged) and press down the dough in order to make the waffle impression.

- Place waffles on a greased baking sheet and bake for 1 hour.

- Cool, and serve each waffle broken into quarters. Store in an airtight container.

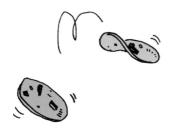

SUNDAY MORNING BEGGIN' CAKES

Makes 8 ooooh!-please-get-up-and-feed-me snacks

HOW CAN YOU SLEEP IN ON A SUNDAY MORNING KNOWING THERE ARE TWO LITTLE BLACK EYES AT THE FOOT OF THE BED, STARING, WAITING, HOPING, PRAYING ...

3 eggs
1¼ cups skim milk
1 tablespoon honey
⅔ cup white flour
¼ cup bacon bits

- In a large bowl, beat eggs until thick, then stir in milk and honey.

- Add sifted flour and bacon bits to the mixture and stir until smooth.

- Drop ¼ cup of the mixture onto a moderately hot greased griddle to make a 6-inch pancake. Turn each pancake when underside is light brown.

- Cool and store in a sealed container in the refrigerator.

Please Don't Litter!

In the US, animal shelters take in some 12 million pets annually. 14% are returned to their owners, 25% are adopted, and the rest are put to sleep—a shocking 7 million pets killed each year.

PLEASE spay or neuter your pet.

GAR"LICKY" FRENCH FRIES

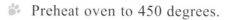

Enough to share with the whole pack

UMMMM ... PAW-TATOES!
RUSTLE UP SOME RUSSETS FOR YOUR JACK RUSSELL

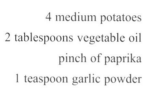

4 medium potatoes
2 tablespoons vegetable oil
pinch of paprika
1 teaspoon garlic powder

- Preheat oven to 450 degrees.

- Peel and cut potatoes into ½-inch strips.

- Toss potato strips in oil and garlic powder and spread on a baking sheet.

- Bake for about 30 minutes, turning several times during cooking until golden.

- Remove from the oven, then sprinkle with a pinch of paprika. Cool before serving. Store in a sealed container and refrigerate.

CORN DOGS

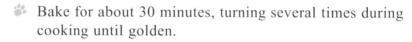

Makes 12 git along little doggies

SO GOOD YOUR DOG WILL "STALK" YOU FOR MORE!

2 cups cornmeal
(white or yellow)
3 tablespoons
vegetable oil
½ cup cooked rice
1 clove garlic, minced
1½ cups water

- Preheat oven to 350 degrees.

- Place cornmeal, oil, cooked rice and garlic in a bowl.

- In a saucepan, bring water to a boil and pour over the cornmeal mixture and stir well.

- Form the mixture into 3-inch patties with your hands.

- Place on a baking sheet and bake for 30 minutes. Cool before serving and store in a sealed container in the refrigerator.

POODLE NOODLES

Makes about 30 impastably yummy noodles

AT LAST, A FRESH AND GREAT-TASTING WAY TO MAKE EATING
SPINACH ALMOST BEARABLE. IT'LL MAKE YOUR DOG STRONG LIKE PUPEYE!

10 ounces frozen chopped spinach
2 eggs
1 clove garlic, minced
1¾ cups white flour

- Thaw and drain spinach and set aside. Combine eggs, garlic and spinach in a blender until smooth.

- Pour into a bowl and gradually add enough flour to make a firm but not sticky dough. Turn out onto a floured surface and knead about 20 times.

- Wrap dough in plastic wrap and leave to rest in the refrigerator for about 30 minutes.

- After dough has rested, roll out on a floured surface to ¹⁄₁₆-inch thick and cut out ½-inch wide noodles. Leave to rest on a clean towel or hang for 1 hour.

- Cook noodles in boiling water until tender, for about 10 to 15 minutes. Drain, cool and serve. Store in a sealed container and refrigerate.

Ciao... Ciao ...Ciao

I-TAIL-IAN MEATBALLS

Makes about 18 ristorante-style meatballs

AMORE! AMORE! THIS CLASSIC ITALIAN CIAO MAKES YOUR DOG FEEL LIKE A STAR—WITHOUT THE PUPARAZZI!

1 pound ground turkey
2 eggs
¼ cup grated Romano cheese
2 cloves garlic, minced
1 tablespoon sweet basil
1 tablespoon parsley flakes
¼ cup bread crumbs

🐾 Mix all ingredients in a large bowl until well blended.

🐾 Roll mixture into balls and fry in a small amount of oil on high heat until the outsides are browned, but not cooked through.

🐾 Turn heat down to low and continue cooking for 20 to 25 minutes. Cool before serving. Store in a sealed container in the refrigerator.

Dottie

The Tax Dog Cometh

Doberman Pinschers got their name from a German tax collector in the 1880s. Ludwig Dobermann, because of the unpopularity of his job (some things never change), developed this especially fierce breed to help him on his rounds. Nice doggie!

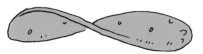

PARLEZ-VOUS PIZZA

Makes 8 universally tasty slices

FRENCH POODLES, ENGLISH SHEEPDOGS AND GERMAN
SHEEPERDS ALL BARK ABOUT THIS DISH—C'EST BONE!

CRUST:

3¼ cups white flour
¼ cup cornmeal
¼ cup vegetable oil
1 egg
1 teaspoon baking soda
1 cup water

TOPPING:

½ cup tomato purée
⅛ cup minced garlic
¼ cup diced mushroom
¼ cup shredded Parmesan cheese
¼ cup shredded mozzarella cheese
1 teaspoon oregano
¼ cup sundried tomatoes

- Preheat oven to 325 degrees.

- To make the crust, mix all ingredients together thoroughly in a large bowl. Turn out onto a lightly floured surface and knead.

- Roll out dough, place on a 10-inch greased pizza pan and bake for about 25 to 30 minutes.

- For the topping, spread the tomato purée evenly on the cooled pizza crust and sprinkle the remaining toppings over the pizza.

- Return to the oven for 20 minutes. Cool and cut into 8 wedges. Store any unused portions in the refrigerator.

FIESTA BONES

Makes 30 get-down-and-pawty crunchers

YIP! YIP! HOORAH! IT'S A BONE-I-FIED CELEBARKTION

1¾ cups water
4 cups whole-wheat flour
½ cup cornmeal
1 egg
2 tablespoons vegetable oil
1 cup sundried tomatoes
1 tablespoon minced garlic
1 tablespoon cilantro
1 tablespoon parsley

- Preheat oven to 375 degrees.

- Combine all ingredients in a large bowl, mixing well, then knead by hand to form a stiff dough.

- Roll out dough to ½-inch thick and cut out bones (or any other shapes) with a 2½-inch cutter.

- Place bones on a greased baking sheet and bake for about 50 minutes. Cool completely before serving and store in an airtight container.

ROOTIN' TOOTIN' WILD WEST CORN MUFFINS

Makes 10 after-the-roundup campfire treats

DOGS LOVE CORN ... SO SCRATCH YOUR COWPOKE BEHIND THE "EARS"
AND SERVE 'EM UP HOT AND TASTY, PAW-DNER

1¾ cups cornmeal

1 teaspoon baking powder

1 teaspoon baking soda

1 tablespoon vegetable shortening

2 eggs

½ cup buttermilk

½ cup skim milk

2 tablespoons honey

½ cup corn

1½ teaspoons rosemary

- Preheat oven to 450 degrees.

- In a large bowl, stir together cornmeal, baking powder, baking soda and shortening.

- In separate bowl, whisk eggs until foamy, then whisk in buttermilk, skim milk and honey.

- Pour wet mixture into the cornmeal mixture and fold in corn and rosemary. Mix well.

- Spoon half full into a greased muffin tin and bake for 10 to 15 minutes until golden and firm. Cool completely, then serve. Store in an airtight container.

SAVORY SCRAPS

Makes 9 scrappily scrumptious squares

IF YOUR DOG INSISTS ON TABLE SCRAPS, HE WON'T BELIEVE HIS LUCK WHEN THIS HITS HIS BOWL!

1 pound ground turkey
1 clove garlic, minced
¼ cup cold water
1 egg, beaten
1 cup cornmeal
1 tablespoon chopped parsley
⅓ cup shredded Parmesan cheese

- 🐾 Preheat oven to 375 degrees.

- 🐾 In a skillet, brown the ground turkey and garlic together, then drain well.

- 🐾 Mix cold water, egg, cornmeal and parsley together in a bowl, then add to the skillet with turkey and garlic.

- 🐾 Cook until thickened, stirring constantly. Cover and continue cooking over low heat for 10 minutes.

- 🐾 Pour into an 8 x 8-inch pan, sprinkle the top with Parmesan cheese and bake for 40 minutes. Cool, cut into 9 squares, then serve. Store well wrapped in the refrigerator.

Cute, and Smart Too

Sarah, Dottie and Gracie are furious that they're not included in the top five smartest breeds:

Border Collie
Poodle
German Shepherd
Golden Retriever
Doberman Pinscher

It's important to remember that holidays can be stressful for your dogs. Increased activity around the house, disruptions to their daily routine, different smells and noises, people rushing about ... it's easy to see how they can feel confused or left out. Try to spend a little extra time playing with your pups or including them in the activities. Pick out your favorite holiday recipe and bake something especially for them. Yappy holidays!

Home for the Holidogs

FLEAS NAVIDAD NIBBLERS

Bakes 16 festive holidog muffins

'TWAS THE NIGHT BEFORE CHRISTMAS AND ALL THROUGH THE HOUSE, NOT A CREATURE WAS STIRRING, EXCEPT FOR THE DOG EATING THESE OFF THE COUNTER ... AS QUIET AS A MOUSE. MERRY DOGMAS!

2 tablespoons honey

2¾ cups water

¼ cup unsweetened applesauce

⅛ teaspoon vanilla

1 egg

½ cup chopped peanuts

4 cups whole-wheat flour

1 tablespoon baking powder

1 tablespoon cinnamon

1 tablespoon nutmeg

- Preheat oven to 350 degrees.

- In a bowl, mix together honey, water, applesauce, vanilla and egg.

- In a separate bowl, mix peanuts, flour, baking powder, cinnamon and nutmeg.

- Add wet ingredients to the dry ingredients and stir, mixing well.

- Spoon into a greased muffin tin, filling each cup two-thirds full. Bake for 35 minutes. Store in a sealed container.

HOWL-O-WEEN TRICKING TREATS

Makes 14 bewitching treats—perfect for gobblin'

THESE FRIGHTFULLY GOOD HOWL-O-WEEN TREATS ARE
GUARANTEED TO GIVE YOUR PUP A VERY
SPOOKY BOO-ST

2½ cups water

½ cup canned pumpkin

⅛ teaspoon vanilla

1 egg

4 cups whole-wheat flour

¼ cup raisins

¼ cup chopped pecans

1 tablespoon baking powder

¼ teaspoon nutmeg

¼ teaspoon cinnamon

¼ cup oats

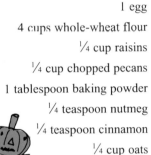

- Preheat oven to 350 degrees.

- In a bowl, mix water, pumpkin, vanilla and egg thoroughly.

- Combine flour, raisins, pecans, baking powder, nutmeg and cinnamon in a separate bowl, stirring well.

- Add wet ingredients to dry and mix well, making sure no dry mixture is left.

- Spoon into a greased muffin tin, filling each cup completely. Sprinkle the top of each muffin with oats and bake for 1¼ hours. Cool completely and store in a sealed container.

No Goblin the Chocolate

Halloween can be even scarier if your dog raids the candy. Chocolate can be extremely toxic to dogs, resulting in anything from an allergic reaction to cardiac arrest. Be sure that all chocolate is safely out of sniffing range.

HANUKKAH NOSHERS

Makes 30 chewish Jewish delights

A PERFECT SNACK FOR ALL ORTHODOGS. MAZEL TOV!

½ cup unsweetened applesauce
1 egg
½ cup natural peanut butter
1 teaspoon vanilla
1¼ cups water
4 cups whole-wheat flour
½ cup cornmeal
½ cup quick-cook oats
¼ cup chopped peanuts

- Preheat oven to 350 degrees.
- In a large mixing bowl, combine applesauce, egg, peanut butter, vanilla and water.
- In a second bowl, combine flour, cornmeal, oats and peanuts.
- Add dry ingredients to wet and mix well.
- Turn dough onto a floured surface and knead until thoroughly mixed together.
- Roll out dough to ¼-inch thick and cut out shapes.
- Place on a greased baking sheet and bake for 45 minutes. Cool on a rack before serving. Store in a sealed container.

YAPPY NEW YEAR YUM YUMS

Makes 12 stroke-of-midnight scrumptious snacks

HELP YOUR DOG KEEP HIS RRRRESOLUTIONS WITH THESE LOW-FAT LIP-SMACKERS

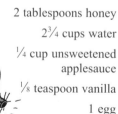

2 tablespoons honey
2¾ cups water
¼ cup unsweetened applesauce
⅛ teaspoon vanilla
1 egg
4 cups whole-wheat flour
1 cup dried apple chips
1 tablespoon baking powder
1 tablespoon cinnamon
1 tablespoon nutmeg

- Preheat oven to 350 degrees.
- In a bowl, mix together honey, water, applesauce, vanilla and egg.
- Combine flour, apple chips, baking powder, cinnamon and nutmeg in a separate bowl and mix thoroughly.
- Add wet ingredients to dry and mix well, scraping sides and bottom of bowl to be sure no dry mixture is left.
- Spoon into greased muffin pans so that each cup is three-quarters full and bake for approximately 1 hour. Cool and store in a sealed container.

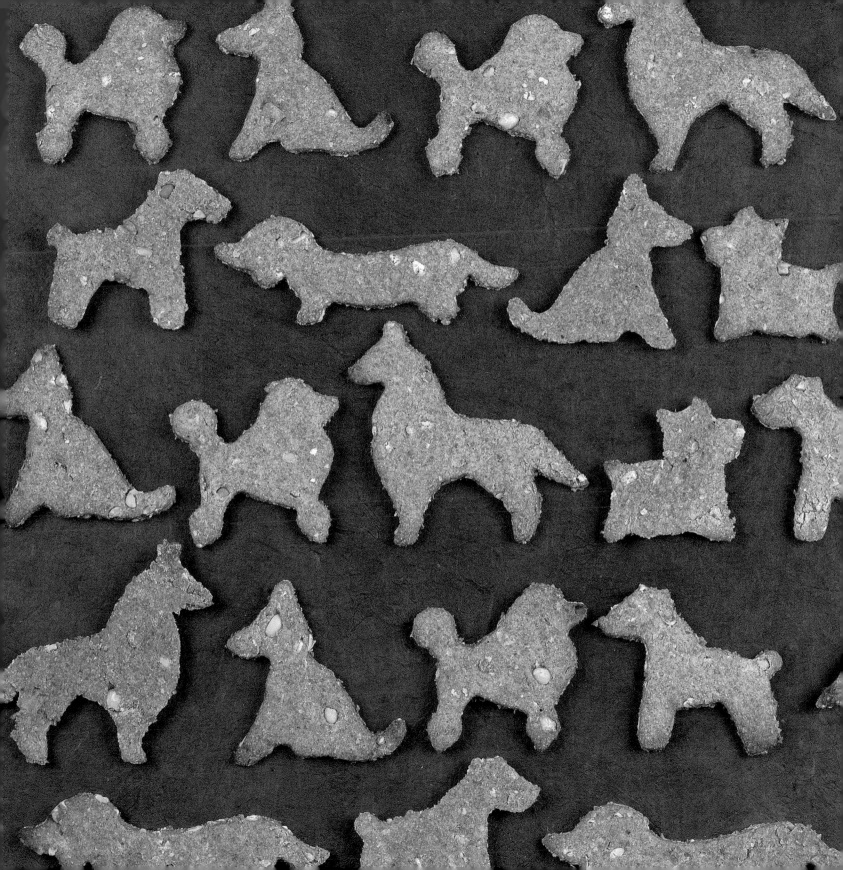

St Patrick's Day Pat-My-Head Pupovers

Bakes 6 top-o'-the-morning treats

'TIS A GLORIOUS THING TO BE AN IRISH WOLFHOUND. TUCK A SHAMROCK IN ME COLLAR, BAKE UP A PUPOVER AND WATCH ME APPETITE'S A-DUBLIN

1 egg

½ cup skim milk

½ cup white flour

½ tablespoon vegetable oil

- Preheat oven to 475 degrees.

- In a mixing bowl, combine eggs, milk and sifted flour and mix thoroughly with an electric beater.

- Add oil and beat for another minute.

- Grease custard cups and fill half full. Bake for 15 minutes, then reduce heat to 350 degrees for an additional 25 to 30 minutes.

- A few minutes before removing from oven, prick each popover with a fork to release the steam. Allow to cool and store in a sealed container in the refrigerator.

THANKSGIVING TURKEY GOBBLERS

Makes 24 tempting, tantalizing turkey treats

YOUR DOG WILL BE GIVING THANKS INDEED WHEN HE GOBBLES DOWN A FEW OF THESE!

1 cup ground turkey
2 cups white flour
1 cup cornmeal
1 egg
3 tablespoons vegetable oil
¾ cup water
2 teaspoons tarragon

- Preheat oven to 375 degrees.

- In a frying pan, cook ground turkey, crumble into small pieces and set aside on a paper towel.

- Combine flour and cornmeal in a large bowl, then in a separate bowl, beat egg, oil and water, then add tarragon.

- Add dry ingredients to wet and mix well. Fold in ground turkey and mix again.

- Turn dough out on a lightly floured surface and knead until thoroughly mixed together. Roll out dough to ½-inch thick and cut out shapes.

- Place on a greased baking sheet and bake for 15 minutes or until firm. Cool and serve. Keep any leftovers in a sealed container in the refrigerator.

Dogs on the Cutting Edge

Put away all knives after use. Your dog can rear his head straight back to sniff out what's on the table, thus facilitating his sword-swallowing act. The New York Animal Medical Center removed an 8-inch blade from the stomach of one pooch patient!

EASTER MORNING HEAVENLY MANNA

Bakes up to 12 squares of saintly goodness

WHETHER YOUR DOG IS A SAINT BERNARD OR A HOLY TERRIER, HE'LL BE PRAYING FOR THESE ON EASTER MORN

6 slices white bread

8 ounces low-fat cream cheese, cubed

4 eggs

1¼ cups skim milk

⅓ cup honey

- Preheat oven to 375 degrees.

- Tear bread slices into cubes and toss lightly with cream cheese cubes.

- Place in an 8 x 8-inch greased baking pan and set aside.

- In a mixing bowl, beat eggs together and add milk and honey. Stir well.

- Pour over bread mixture and bake for 30 minutes. Cool, then cut into squares. Store leftovers well wrapped in the refrigerator.

MUTTHER'S DAY PUPPY SEED BREAD

Makes 12 slices—enough for the whole litter

IT'S MUTTHER'S DAY! SHE'LL LOVE TO LOAF ALL DAY ENJOYING THIS DELICIOUS BREAD!

3 cups white flour

1 teaspoon baking powder

¾ cup honey

1½ cups skim milk

1 egg

½ cup natural peanut butter

⅓ cup vegetable oil

1 teaspoon poppy seeds

1½ teaspoons vanilla

1 teaspoon almond extract

- Preheat oven to 350 degrees.

- Combine all ingredients in a large bowl and mix thoroughly.

- Pour mixture into a greased loaf pan and bake for 50 minutes, or until a toothpick comes out clean when inserted into the middle.

- Cool before serving in slices. Wrap any leftovers tightly and store.

ST VALENTINE'S DAY FRISKY FEAST

Makes 16 moonstruck muffins

WHETHER IT'S A ROMANTIC ROTTWEILER RENDEZVOUS OR A LUSTY LATE-NIGHT LABRADOR LIAISON, THESE ARE THE IDEAL MATES FOR CANOODLING CANINES

1½ cups whole-wheat flour
1 cup rolled oats
1 cup oat bran
2 teaspoons baking soda
1 teaspoon cinnamon
2 apples, peeled and diced
½ cup raisins
1 egg
¼ cup honey
3 tablespoons vegetable oil
¼ cup walnuts
1 cup skim milk

- Preheat oven to 400 degrees.
- In a bowl, combine flour, oats, oat bran, baking soda and cinnamon.
- Add apples, raisins, egg, honey, oil and walnuts. Stir thoroughly.
- Add milk and mix thoroughly.
- Spoon batter into a greased muffin tin so that cups are three-quarters full and bake for 20 to 25 minutes. Cool before serving and store in a sealed container.

GINGER'S FOURTH OF JULY SNAPS

Makes 18 crispy, crunchy summertime snacks

MAKING THESE COOKIES IS A SNAP—
AND THE RESULTS WILL BE EXPLOSIVE!

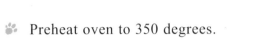

½ cup molasses
2 tablespoons honey
½ cup water
¼ cup vegetable oil
3 cups white flour
1 teaspoon baking soda
¼ teaspoon cinnamon
½ teaspoon ground cloves
2 tablespoons ground ginger
¼ cup raisins
¼ cup chopped pecans

- Preheat oven to 350 degrees.

- In a bowl, combine molasses, honey, water and oil.

- In another bowl, mix flour, baking soda, cinnamon, cloves, ginger, raisins and pecans. Stir dry mixture into wet and mix well.

- On a lightly floured surface knead and roll out dough to ¼-inch thick, then cut out shapes.

- Place on a greased baking sheet and bake for 20 minutes. Cool on a rack then store in a sealed container.

DoTTie

In-the-pen-dence Day

Firecrackers can turn your pup into a raging terror. Keep pets indoors and comfort them with treats and extra love. This is called densensitization—introducing your dog to scary situations, then rewarding him positively.

Celebrations can come at any time or any place—your pooch's birthday, a welcome home celebration from the kennel or vet, or for graduating from obedience school ... One of the great things about dogs is that they live very much for the moment. What's done is past and forgotten and they have no concept of the future, so each moment is filled with living now. So why not start celebrating those meaningful moments in life—however big or small—by baking up a special treat! And be sure to invite us!

BATH BRIBES

Makes 10 water-free, after-bath rewards

SPLISH ... SPLASH ... I HATE BATHS!
SCRUB-A-DUB-DUB FEED YOUR DOG IN THE TUB

Ingredients	Instructions

1 egg

1¼ cups skim milk

¼ cup vegetable oil

1½ teaspoons baking powder

½ teaspoon baking soda

1½ cups whole-wheat flour

½ cup bran flakes

½ cup raisins

¼ cup pecans

- Preheat oven to 375 degrees.

- In a mixing bowl, combine egg, milk and oil.

- Stir in baking powder, baking soda, flour and bran flakes. Mix well, then fold in raisins and pecans.

- Spoon into a greased muffin tin so that cups are three-quarters full and bake for 25 minutes. Cool before serving and store in a sealed container.

NEW DIGS PIE

Cuts up into 8 scoffable servings

WELCOME TO THE DOGHOUSE!
YOUR NEW POOCH WILL FEEL RIGHT AT HOME
WITH THIS MADE-FROM-SCRATCH PAWSTRY

CRUST:

1½ cups white flour

½ cup vegetable shortening

4–5 tablespoons cold water

FILLING:

3 tablespoons white flour

½ cup honey

2 cups skim milk

4 egg yolks

½ cup natural peanut butter

1 teaspoon parsley

- Preheat oven to 450 degrees.

- To make the crust, sift flour into a medium bowl and cut in shortening until pieces are the size of small peas.

- Sprinkle 1 tablespoon water at a time over the mixture and gently toss with a fork until it forms into a ball.

- Roll out pastry on a lightly floured surface to fit into an 8-inch pie plate and trim the edges. Bake for 10 to 12 minutes then leave to cool.

- To make the filling, put all ingredients in a blender and whizz until smooth.

- Pour into a saucepan and cook over medium heat until thick. Cool and pour into the baked pie shell. Refrigerate until set and store any leftovers in the refrigerator.

How Old in Dog Years?

The world's oldest dog was an Australian Cattle Dog called Bluey. He was obtained as a puppy in 1910 and worked actively for almost 20 years. He was put to sleep in 1939 at the age of 29 years. May all our dogs be so lucky!

71

WELCOME HOME KENNEL CAKES

Makes 12 good-to-be-home treats

WHAT BETTER WAY TO SAY YOU'RE SORRY FOR SENDING YOUR COLLIE TO THE KENNEL?

4 cups oat bran
2½ cups white flour
2½ teaspoons baking soda
1 egg
½ cup vegetable oil
½ cup honey
½ cup natural peanut butter
2½ cups buttermilk

- Preheat oven to 375 degrees.

- Mix oat bran, flour and baking soda in a large bowl. Add egg, oil, honey, peanut butter and buttermilk and stir.

- Fill a greased muffin tin so that cups are two-thirds full and bake for 25 minutes or until a toothpick comes out clean when inserted into the center.

- Serve when cooled and store in a sealed container.

BOW VOWS AMOUR CAKE

Makes an 8-inch wedding night delight

A BLISSFUL UNION OF CREAM CHEESE AND HONEY
... ESPECIALLY FOR THE MARRIAGE-MINDED MUTT

8 ounces low-fat cream cheese
¾ cup honey
1 tablespoon cornstarch
2 eggs
1½ teaspoons vanilla
½ cup sliced almonds

- Preheat over to 350 degrees.

- Beat cream cheese with an electric blender until smooth, then beat in honey until blended.

- Sprinkle in cornstarch while using the mixer on low speed. Add eggs and vanilla and beat until well blended.

- Pour into an 8-inch greased spring-form pan and bake for 35 minutes or until the edges of the cake are lightly browned. Turn out of the pan and cool on a rack.

- Garnish the cake with sliced almonds and store in a sealed container.

GRADUATION GOOD DOG GOODIES

Makes 25 best-behavior teacher's tidbits

YOUR POOCH WILL GRADUATE WAGNA CUM LAUDE FOR THESE LUSCIOUS BARS!

4 cups whole-wheat flour

½ cup cornmeal

1 egg

¼ cup natural peanut butter

1¾ cups water

FILLING:

12 ounces low-fat cream cheese

1 teaspoon vanilla

- Preheat oven to 350 degrees.

- Mix together flour, cornmeal, egg, peanut butter and water in a large bowl and stir.

- Turn out onto a lightly floured surface and knead until thoroughly mixed into a ball of dough.

- Roll out the dough to about ⅛-inch thick and cut out rectangles 6 inches long and 1½ inches wide.

- Place on a greased baking sheet and bake for 45 minutes.

- After bars have cooled on a rack, mix the filling together and spread a small amount between two bars and press together. Store in a sealed container in the refrigerator.

- Variation: replace the peanut butter with ¼ cup carob chips, or alternatively with ¼ cup chopped sundried tomatoes, 1 tablespoon oregano and 1 tablespoon minced garlic.

PARTY HEARTY MIX-IT-UP MIX

Makes 42 hellraisin', raucous, rowdy snacks

THE FAVORITE FOR SQUIRREL-CHASIN', STICK-FETCHIN', HOLE-DIGGIN' HOUNDS—LET THE GOOD TIMES ROLL-OVER!

½ cup vegetable oil
½ cup honey
1 teaspoon vanilla
1 egg
4 teaspoons skim milk
2½ cups whole-wheat flour
1 teaspoon baking powder
½ teaspoon ground ginger

- Preheat oven to 375 degrees.

- Mix together oil, honey, vanilla, egg and milk in a bowl.

- In a separate bowl, blend together flour, baking powder and ginger.

- Combine dry ingredients with wet mixture and stir thoroughly.

- Knead the dough on a lightly floured surface, roll out to ¼-inch thick and cut into shapes.

- Place on a greased cookie sheet and bake for 15 minutes. Cool on a rack and store in an airtight container.

Who's the Boss?

Avoid dominance-provoking games such as tug-of-war, wrestling and chasing. These games encourage aggression and biting.
Play games such as fetch and frisbee instead, to establish a positive relationship with your dog.

DoTtie

LET 'EM EAT CAKE

Makes 8 devouringly-good slices of pawty cake

IT'S WORTH HAVING SEVEN BIRTHDAYS A YEAR FOR THIS CAKE!

2 cups water
¼ cup mashed banana
⅛ teaspoon vanilla
1 egg
2 tablespoons honey
3 cups whole-wheat flour
1 cup dried bananas
½ tablespoon baking powder

FROSTING:
8 ounces low-fat cream cheese
3 teaspoons carob powder
1 teaspoon vanilla

- Preheat oven to 350 degrees.
- In a bowl, mix together water, bananas, vanilla, egg and honey.
- In a separate bowl, combine flour, dried bananas and baking powder. Mix thoroughly.
- Add wet ingredients to dry and mix well.
- Pour into an 8-inch greased cake pan and bake for 45 minutes or until a toothpick inserted into the center comes out clean.
- To make the frosting, beat all ingredients together in a small bowl until smooth.
- Spread over the cake and decorate it with pieces of crushed dried banana. Store in an airtight container.

DOCTOR FEELGOOD'S FEEL BETTER MUFFINS

Makes 18 extra-love, feel-better treats

SEND TAIL-WAGGING WISHES FOR A SPEEDY RECOVERY!

1 cup cooked rice
1 cup skim milk
2 tablespoons vegetable oil
1 cup white flour
1 tablespoon baking powder
1 clove garlic, minced
3 egg whites

- Preheat oven to 350 degrees.
- In a bowl, combine cooked rice, milk and oil.
- Add flour, baking powder and garlic, stirring well.
- In a separate bowl, beat egg whites until stiff then fold into the rice mixture.
- Spoon into a muffin tin so that cups are half full and bake for 25 minutes. Cool before serving and store in an airtight container.

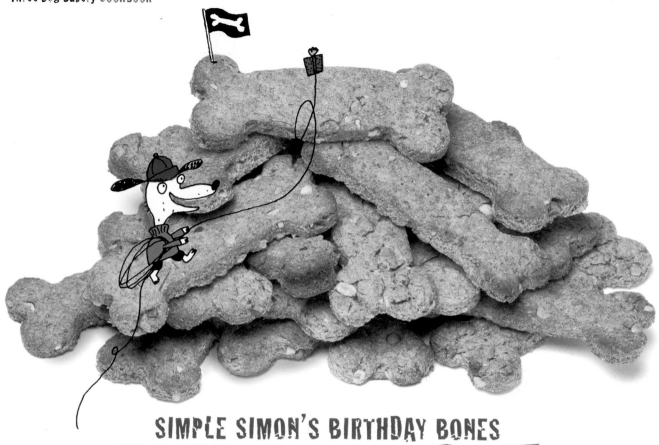

SIMPLE SIMON'S BIRTHDAY BONES

Makes 30 large bone-bones

SIMON SAYS, "STOP!" "SNIFF!" "DROOL!" "MUNCH!" "CRUNCH!" "WAG!"
BIRTHDAY BONES FOR ALL!

2 cups whole-wheat flour
1 tablespoon baking powder
1 cup natural peanut butter
1 cup skim milk

Preheat oven to 375 degrees.

In a bowl, combine flour and baking powder. In another bowl, mix peanut butter and milk.

Add wet mixture to dry, and mix well.

Turn out dough on a lightly floured surface and knead. Roll out to ¼-inch thick and cut out shapes.

Place on a greased baking sheet and bake for 20 minutes or until lightly brown. Cool on a rack then store in an airtight container.

BARK MITZVAH SQUARES

Bakes up 18 squares—enough to share with the whole synodog

OY VEH! COMING OF AGE NEVER TASTED SO GOOD!
THIS RECIPE ISRAEL GOOD!

½ cup vegetable shortening
⅛ cup honey
4 eggs
1 teaspoon vanilla
¼ cup carob powder
1 cup white flour
½ teaspoon baking powder
½ cup carob chips

FROSTING:
8 ounces low-fat cream cheese
3 teaspoons carob powder
1 teaspoon vanilla

- Preheat oven to 350 degrees.

- In a large bowl, cream shortening and honey together thoroughly.

- Add eggs, vanilla, carob powder, flour, baking powder and carob chips. Beat well.

- Bake in a greased 9 x 13 inch baking sheet for 25 minutes, then allow to cool.

- To make the frosting, mix cream cheese, carob powder and vanilla in a bowl.

- Spread over cooled brownies then cut into squares. Cover unused portion with plastic wrap or store in a sealed container in the refrigerator.

Gleaming Growls

When your puppy reaches full doghood, he will have 42 permanent teeth. Dogs can suffer from tartar build up, cavities and tooth loss. So to keep his fangs gleaming, feed him dry and crunchy food and brush his teeth once a week.

Index

Sarah, Dottie and Gracie's trivia facts on the following pages are from these sources: p.13 *The 1998 Guinness Book of Records*; p.23 *The New York Times*; p.27 *The Reader's Digest Book of Facts*; p.31 American Kennel Club; p.35 *1996 National Pet Survey*; p.39 *The Guinness Book of Pet Records*; p.47 The Humane Society of the United States; p.51 *The Reader's Digest Book of Facts*; p.55 *The Intelligence of Dogs* by Stanley Coren; p.71 *The 1998 Guinness Book of Records*.

doggie donuts
GRACIE'S GREAT DANISH
DOTTIES DIPPED DELIGHTS
BONES TO GO
BROWNIES
thanks!
dottie
Bone Appetit
SHAKE
Fig. 32
SIT
Page 7
HEART
TRICKS TO GET YOU TREATS.
VOL. I
SPEAK
Page 14
ROLL-OVER
Fig. 22
Ribs
PIZZA
BARK BARK
BARKIN' FOR BROWNIES
A REAL TAIL-WAGGER